A Year of Gratitude Journal

A YEAR OF
Gratitude
JOURNAL

52 Weeks of Prompts and
Exercises to Cultivate Positivity
and Joy // KEIR BRADY MS, LMFT

ROCKRIDGE
PRESS

To Charley, Alyssa, Evan, and Liam for giving me so many reasons to be grateful

Interior and Cover Designer: Lisa Schreiber
Art Producer: Samantha Ulban
Editor: Crystal Nero
Production Editor: Emily Sheehan
Production Manager: Riley Hoffman

All Illustrations used under license © West Wind Creative/Creative Market. Author Photo Courtesy of Christina Tyler Photography.

ISBN: Print 978-1-64876-729-6
R0

This journal belongs to

_____

Introduction

In my work as a marriage and family therapist, I've noticed that practicing gratitude makes a big difference in a person's quality of life, relationships, and ability to find a sense of inner peace. Gratitude refers to a feeling of thankfulness and an expression of appreciation for who you are, what you have, and what other people have done for you. When you practice gratitude, you focus on everything good in your life. Focusing on the positives means thinking about everything that is going well instead of ruminating on your fears, regrets, and problems.

Saying thank you to a stranger who holds the door open for you, letting your child know how much you enjoyed their hug, and being thankful for the ability to hug your child back are all ways of expressing gratitude. This can enhance your mood and improve your emotional well-being—it's hard to focus on negative feelings when you're conscious of all of your blessings.

Keeping a journal is a good way to consistently practice gratitude. Regularly writing down all the things you are grateful for helps increase feelings of positivity and happiness, improves self-esteem, and makes managing stress easier. A gratitude journal practice is a good reminder to focus on the positive because it allows you to either begin or end your day by writing down the things that bring you joy and happiness. It's something that I often suggest to my clients, and I keep my own gratitude journal, too.

By practicing gratitude daily, you can experience many beneficial changes in your life. According to a study by

Emmons and McCullough, people who wrote about things that they were grateful for that had occurred during the week felt better about their lives and were more optimistic than those in the study who didn't. Cultivating gratitude can also help you sleep better and improve your physical health. The Thnx4.org project found that, after two weeks, those who participated in their online gratitude journal had fewer headaches, improved skin, reduced congestion, and less stomach pain.

A regular gratitude practice can improve your interpersonal relationships, too. Expressing appreciation for your partner creates a more peaceful, loving environment where you focus on positive things, which makes it easier to find forgiveness. When working with couples, I've noticed that when each person starts writing in a gratitude journal, their arguments decrease and their relationship satisfaction increases.

Best of all, the more you practice gratitude, the more you want to practice gratitude. That's because it releases the feel-good neurotransmitters serotonin and dopamine, which create positive feelings that motivate you to repeat these behaviors. A study by Grant and Gino found that gratitude leads to prosocial behavior, which benefits not only the individual but society as a whole. So as you embark on this year-long journey of gratitude, remember that you'll not only feel the benefits of this practice now, but you will also feel its impact on your life far into the future.

The ache for home lives in all of us, the safe place where we can go as we are and not be questioned.

MAYA ANGELOU

Where in your home do you feel most comfortable and like yourself? Why?

_____

_____

_____

_____

_____

_____

_____

_____

_____

_____

_____

_____

What is your favorite thing to do in this place, and what do you like
about it?

_____

_____

_____

_____

_____

_____

Describe a happy memory of this place and how you feel when you
think about it.

_____

_____

_____

_____

_____

_____

_____

_____

_____

_____

_____

_____

Go to this place in your home and engage all of your senses. What do you see? Can you smell anything? What are you touching? What do you hear? Do you taste anything? Take a deep breath in and notice the feelings that come up. As you breathe out, remind yourself that you can experience these wonderful feelings whenever you want, just by thinking about this special place.

> I am grateful for my body and all of the amazing things it can do.

What is one thing you love about your body and why?

_____

_____

_____

_____

_____

_____

_____

_____

_____

_____

_____

_____

_____

_____

_____

My favorite way to move my body is . . .

_____

_____

_____

_____

_____

_____

Is there a body part you sometimes take for granted? Write down all of the reasons why this body part is so important to you.

_____

_____

_____

_____

_____

_____

_____

_____

_____

_____

Lie down on your back in a comfortable place. Starting with your toes, tense and release your muscles by squeezing tightly as you breathe in, and letting go as you breathe out. Then, move on to your feet, legs, glutes, abdomen, back, hands, arms, shoulders, and neck before ending with your face. As you do this, think about something you can be grateful for about each body part.

There is nothing on this earth more to be prized than true friendship.

— ST. THOMAS AQUINAS

What activities do you love to do with your friends, and why do you love doing them with those people in particular?

_____

_____

_____

_____

_____

_____

_____

_____

_____

_____

_____

_____

_____

_____

Why are your friends so important to you?

_____

_____

_____

_____

_____

_____

_____

Write a letter to a friend who helped you through a difficult time. Tell them what they did for you and how much you appreciate them.

_____

_____

_____

_____

_____

_____

_____

_____

_____

_____

_____

Plan a special day with your friend in which you do something that you both enjoy. Try to pick something that allows you time to chat, so that you can let them know how grateful you are for their friendship and share the letter you wrote them. This could be cooking a meal together, going for a hike, or wandering through an art gallery.

> I am in awe of the beauty
> I see all around me.

Name 10 things that you can see around you now that you are grateful for and explain why you are grateful for them.

_____

_____

_____

_____

_____

_____

_____

_____

_____

_____

_____

_____

_____

_____

_____

_____

What is something that you look forward to seeing every day? How does it make you feel when you see it?

_____

_____

_____

_____

_____

_____

_____

_____

Think of one of the most beautiful things you have ever seen. Describe it in detail.

_____

_____

_____

_____

_____

_____

_____

_____

_____

This week, when you are out and about, pay attention to the things that you see. Each day, find one thing that you never really noticed before and express gratitude for it. Reflect on how focusing on these things shifts your mood and how it makes you feel. For example, do you feel more optimistic or less stressed?

Live in each season as it passes; breathe the air, drink the drink, taste the fruit, and resign yourself to the influence of the earth.

— HENRY DAVID THOREAU

Which season of the year do you like best, and why are you grateful when it arrives?

_____

_____

_____

_____

_____

_____

_____

_____

_____

_____

_____

_____

What activity do you most enjoy doing during this season? Explain what you like most about this activity.

_____

_____

_____

_____

_____

_____

_____

_____

Now think about the other seasons. Are there things you like about those, too? For each season, make a list of three things that you are grateful for that you usually overlook during those times of the year.

_____

_____

_____

_____

_____

_____

_____

_____

_____

One morning or evening this week, find some quiet time when you can sit down and relax. Close your eyes and imagine a perfect day during your favorite season. Are you inside or outside? What is the weather like? What are you doing? Who is with you? What are you feeling? What do you notice? When you are ready, open your eyes and allow the feelings to stay with you.

> I have overcome challenges before,
> and I know I can do it again.

When I am faced with a challenge, I . . .

_____

_____

_____

_____

_____

_____

_____

_____

_____

_____

_____

_____

_____

_____

_____

An important lesson I learned from a challenge I faced was ...

_____

_____

_____

_____

_____

_____

_____

_____

Think about something you have in your life now that you are grateful for, but that you wouldn't have if you hadn't endured a challenge first. Perhaps it's a qualification, a skill, a job title, or a fitness level. What was the hardest part of that challenge, and how did you overcome it?

_____

_____

_____

_____

_____

_____

_____

Visualize a challenge that you are facing now. Think about the steps that are needed to overcome this challenge and imagine yourself navigating those steps successfully. What did you notice from this visualization? Is there anything you learned that can help you address this challenge now?

Always laugh when you can. It is cheap medicine.

— LORD BYRON

My funniest memory is ...

_____

_____

_____

_____

_____

_____

_____

_____

_____

_____

_____

_____

_____

_____

Whenever I need a good laugh, I ...

_____

_____

_____

_____

_____

_____

Write about an experience that didn't seem funny at the time, but makes you laugh out loud whenever you think about it now. Why are you grateful for that memory?

_____

_____

_____

_____

_____

_____

_____

_____

_____

_____

Try to do something that makes you laugh each day this week. It can be as simple as watching a short, social media video or listening to a funny podcast or radio show. If you have more time, you can watch a funny movie, call a childhood friend and reminisce about all of the fun you had, or read a humorous book or comic. Let yourself laugh out loud and think about how your body feels afterward. Are you more relaxed? Do you feel less stressed? Are you finding that you laugh more easily in general at the end of the week? Note these observations.

> My childhood may not have been perfect, but I do have some very fond memories.

What was one thing in your childhood that you couldn't live without and why?

_____

_____

_____

_____

_____

_____

_____

_____

_____

_____

_____

_____

_____

_____

My favorite childhood memory is . . .

_____

_____

_____

_____

_____

_____

_____

If you could go back in time as an adult and talk to yourself as a child, what would you tell yourself to really pay attention to and why?

_____

_____

_____

_____

_____

_____

_____

_____

_____

_____

_____

This week, take some time to look at old photographs of yourself at different times in your childhood. Think about what was going on when each one was taken—things that you might not be able to see in the actual photograph. What were you feeling at that time? What was something during that time that felt challenging but that you are grateful for now?

Home is people. Not a place.

— ROBIN HOBB

What makes someone feel like family to you, regardless of whether they are actually related to you?

_____

_____

_____

_____

_____

_____

_____

_____

_____

_____

_____

_____

_____

_____

What is the best advice you ever got from an important family figure who helped raise you?

_____

_____

_____

_____

_____

_____

Write a letter to someone who helped guide you in your life when you were younger, thanking them for everything they have done for you.

_____

_____

_____

_____

_____

_____

_____

_____

_____

Share your letter with this person and let them know how much they mean to you. If this isn't possible, read it out loud to yourself or think about how you can do something to honor them this week, based on the lessons they taught you.

Crying is a sign of inner
strength, not weakness.

I am moved to tears by...

_____

_____

_____

_____

_____

_____

_____

_____

_____

_____

_____

_____

_____

_____

_____

Whenever I need a good cry, I . . .

_____

_____

_____

_____

_____

_____

_____

_____

Think about the last time you had a good cry. Write down what was going on and how you felt during and after crying.

_____

_____

_____

_____

_____

_____

_____

_____

_____

Art and culture can often help us get in touch with our emotions. What is a song, book, movie, or video that moves you to tears whenever you hear, read, or watch it? Find a comfortable place where you can be alone and engage with that thing, noticing how it makes you feel. What about it do you find so touching? Lean into the feeling and allow the tears to flow for as long as they need to.

In all things of nature there is something of the marvelous.

— ARISTOTLE

When I think of nature, I think of . . .

_____

_____

_____

_____

_____

_____

_____

_____

_____

_____

_____

_____

_____

_____

What is your favorite way to experience nature? What do you like about it?

_____

_____

_____

_____

_____

_____

_____

_____

Reflect on one thing in nature that you are grateful for. Write down as many reasons as you can, describing why you are grateful for this.

_____

_____

_____

_____

_____

_____

_____

_____

_____

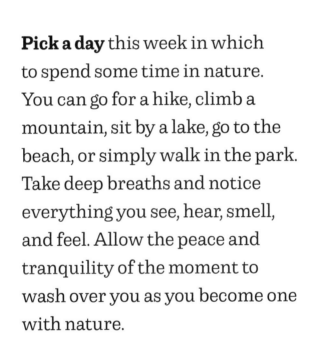

Pick a day this week in which to spend some time in nature. You can go for a hike, climb a mountain, sit by a lake, go to the beach, or simply walk in the park. Take deep breaths and notice everything you see, hear, smell, and feel. Allow the peace and tranquility of the moment to wash over you as you become one with nature.

> I enjoy doing kind things for others because it makes me feel good, too.

The nicest thing a stranger has done for me was . . .

_____

_____

_____

_____

_____

_____

_____

_____

_____

_____

_____

_____

_____

An act of kindness I witnessed was . . .

_____

_____

_____

_____

_____

_____

_____

_____

_____

Write about a time that you did something nice for a stranger and how it made you feel.

_____

_____

_____

_____

_____

_____

_____

_____

_____

Each day this week, think of one random act of kindness that you can do for someone you don't know. It can be a small thing, like giving up your seat on the bus, buying someone in need a coffee, or writing an anonymous thank-you note. Think about how you feel while planning it and how you feel when you do it. How could you make this a more regular practice in your life?

Our chief want in life is somebody who will make us do what we can.

— RALPH WALDO EMERSON

What is the best advice you have ever received from a mentor?

_____

_____

_____

_____

_____

_____

_____

_____

_____

_____

_____

_____

_____

_____

_____

In what area of your life could you play the role of a mentor and why?

_____

_____

_____

_____

_____

_____

_____

_____

Who was your greatest mentor? Explain why you admire them and how they have shaped you as a person.

_____

_____

_____

_____

_____

_____

_____

_____

_____

_____

Call or email a mentor you had in the past and tell them why you are grateful for them. Then, as you go about your week, think about someone in your life who might benefit from your guidance as a way of paying it forward. It doesn't need to be a huge investment of your time or an ongoing mentor relationship, but maybe there is someone who could benefit from your advice or even a few words of encouragement.

> ## I have the skills and knowledge I need to be successful in my work.

What do you like most about what you do for work, and what makes you good at what you do?

_____

_____

_____

_____

_____

_____

_____

_____

_____

_____

_____

_____

_____

_____

What are you most proud of in your professional life and why?

_____

_____

_____

_____

_____

_____

_____

_____

Describe your ideal job. What does it involve doing? What do you like most about it? Why is it perfect for you?

_____

_____

_____

_____

_____

_____

_____

_____

_____

_____

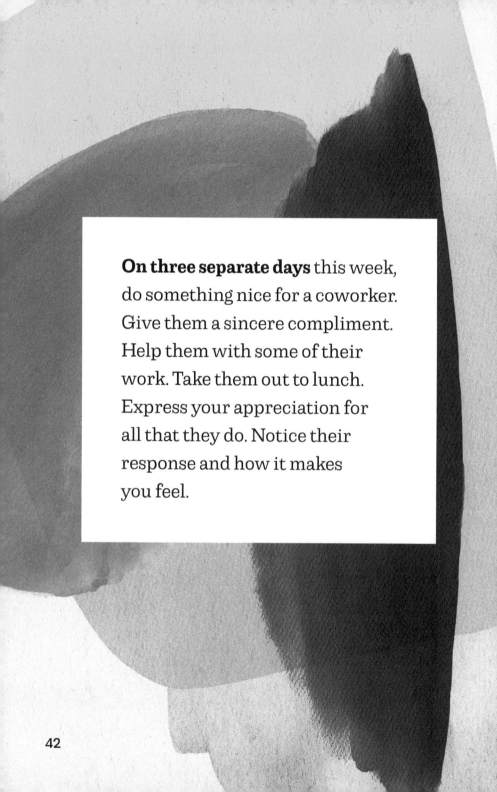

On three separate days this week, do something nice for a coworker. Give them a sincere compliment. Help them with some of their work. Take them out to lunch. Express your appreciation for all that they do. Notice their response and how it makes you feel.

Everyone thinks of changing the world, but no one thinks of changing himself.

— LEO TOLSTOY

Change makes me feel ... because ...

_____

_____

_____

_____

_____

_____

_____

_____

_____

_____

_____

_____

_____

What is one of the best changes you have made in your life and why?

_____

_____

_____

_____

_____

_____

_____

_____

Describe a time when you had to adjust to a big change. What happened? Was this a positive or negative situation? What did you learn from this experience?

_____

_____

_____

_____

_____

_____

_____

_____

Think about a positive change you need to make in your life. Do you need to be kinder to yourself? Do you need to break a bad habit? What about letting go of a grudge, or working toward a goal? Each day this week, take a small step closer to making that change. At the end of the week, think about how it felt to actively focus on changing something.

I embrace the growth that comes with new experiences.

What was the most exciting experience you've ever had and why?

_____

_____

_____

_____

_____

_____

_____

_____

_____

_____

_____

_____

_____

_____

_____

_____

_____

When I experience something new and unfamiliar, I feel...

_____

_____

_____

_____

_____

_____

_____

_____

Write about one of your most interesting experiences. What happened? What did you learn from it? Would you ever want to do it again? Why or why not?

_____

_____

_____

_____

_____

_____

_____

_____

_____

Choose one day during this week to try something new. It can be something simple like trying a new food or taking a different route to work, or it can be something more challenging like signing up for a class to learn a new skill. After you do this, think about how it felt when you were planning it and how it felt when you completed it. Describe what this was like for you.

Emotions are celebrated and repressed, analyzed and medicated, adored and ignored— but rarely, if ever, are they honored.

— KARLA MCLAREN

How do you recognize and honor your feelings?

_____

_____

_____

_____

_____

_____

_____

_____

_____

_____

_____

_____

_____

_____

What emotions can be challenging for you to recognize and why?

_____

_____

_____

_____

_____

_____

_____

Think about a time when you were able to understand and accept a difficult feeling you were experiencing. You might have felt sad, worried, angry, or embarrassed. What was it like recognizing and honoring this feeling?

_____

_____

_____

_____

_____

_____

_____

_____

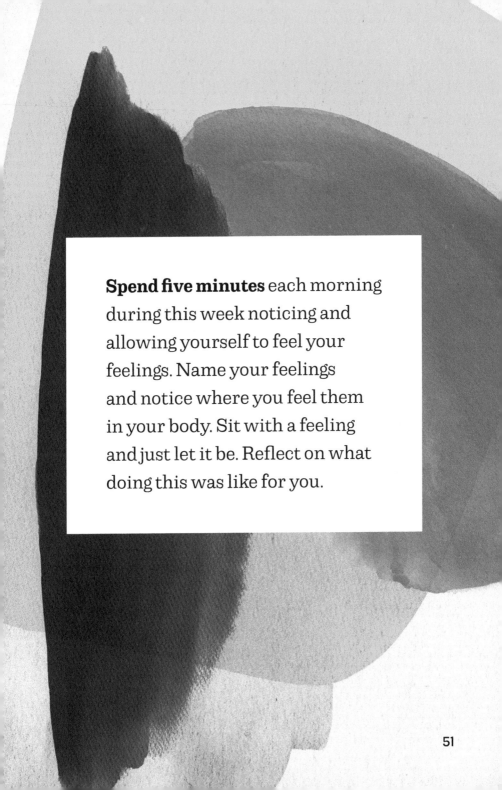

Spend five minutes each morning during this week noticing and allowing yourself to feel your feelings. Name your feelings and notice where you feel them in your body. Sit with a feeling and just let it be. Reflect on what doing this was like for you.

I support my body, mind, and spirit by making healthy choices.

I feel healthiest when I . . .

_____

_____

_____

_____

_____

_____

_____

_____

_____

_____

_____

_____

_____

_____

What are some things you can do every day to maintain a healthy lifestyle?

_____

_____

_____

_____

_____

_____

_____

Think of a time when you were working through a health challenge. Explain what it was like, what you had to do to get better, what you put in place to remain healthy once you recovered, and how it felt to overcome it.

_____

_____

_____

_____

_____

_____

_____

Prioritize one healthy habit this week. This can include cooking healthy dinners, exercising daily, going to bed at the same time every night, or even simply drinking more water. What was doing this like for you? Is it something you would like to continue?

Animals are such agreeable friends—they ask no questions, they pass no criticisms.

— GEORGE ELIOT

What was your favorite childhood pet and why? This can include a family member's pet, neighbor's pet, or even an imaginary pet you had as a child.

_____

_____

_____

_____

_____

_____

_____

_____

_____

_____

_____

_____

_____

_____

I am grateful for my pet or a pet I know because . . .

_____

_____

_____

_____

_____

_____

_____

Think of a time when a pet was there for you during a period of transition. How did they help you?

_____

_____

_____

_____

_____

_____

_____

_____

_____

Spend time with your pet, or a pet belonging to a friend or family member. Plan what you will do together, even if it's just going for a walk or snuggling up on the sofa. Think of how good it feels to be in the presence of such unconditional love. Shower this pet with affection and notice how the quality time with them shifts your mood.

> I am grateful for the food
> that nourishes my body.

What is your favorite food, and why do you like it so much?

_____

_____

_____

_____

_____

_____

_____

_____

_____

_____

_____

_____

_____

_____

_____

What food brings up a special memory for you? What is the memory?

_____

_____

_____

_____

_____

_____

_____

_____

Describe a family tradition around food. What do you eat? Who makes it? Why is it special to you?

_____

_____

_____

_____

_____

_____

_____

_____

_____

_____

This week, make some of your favorite things to eat. Follow a recipe that you loved as a child or recreate one of your favorite meals. Make something that always brings you comfort or reminds you of home. Invite a friend or family member to enjoy it with you and think about how grateful you are to be able to share this food with your loved ones.

I love to be alone. I never found the companion that was so companionable as solitude.

— HENRY DAVID THOREAU

When I am alone, I like to . . .

_____

_____

_____

_____

_____

_____

_____

_____

_____

_____

_____

_____

_____

_____

_____

I look forward to alone time because it makes me feel . . .

_____

_____

_____

_____

_____

_____

_____

If you had an entire day to spend all alone, what would you do? Plan your day.

_____

_____

_____

_____

_____

_____

_____

_____

Spend time alone each day this week. Think about what you want to do during this time and why it's important to you. Maybe you'd like to read a book, watch a movie, take a long bath, or do something artistic like drawing. How do you feel about setting aside time just for you? How is doing this helpful to you—and to your loved ones as well?

I can acknowledge my faults and forgive myself, and I am able to forgive others as well.

What does forgiveness mean to you?

_____

_____

_____

_____

_____

_____

_____

_____

_____

_____

_____

_____

_____

_____

Describe a time someone hurt you and you were able to forgive them.

_____

_____

_____

_____

_____

_____

_____

Think about a time when someone forgave you. What happened? How did you feel when they were able to forgive you?

_____

_____

_____

_____

_____

_____

_____

_____

_____

Think about something or someone you have struggled to forgive. Is there a way you can start the process of forgiveness now? What does this mean to you? How is forgiveness beneficial to your emotional well-being? If you choose to forgive, note how it makes you feel.

It is not our differences that divide us. It is our inability to recognize, accept, and celebrate those differences.

— AUDRE LORDE

Is there someone in your life who is very different from you? It could be a family member, friend, coworker, or neighbor. What makes them different?

_____

_____

_____

_____

_____

_____

_____

_____

_____

_____

_____

_____

_____

What is one valuable thing that you have learned from someone who has a different opinion about something you feel strongly about?

_____

_____

_____

_____

_____

_____

Think of a time in your life when you felt different from everyone else, perhaps when you moved to a new town or started a new job. How did that make you feel, and how did it help you appreciate your differences and turn them into strengths?

_____

_____

_____

_____

_____

_____

_____

_____

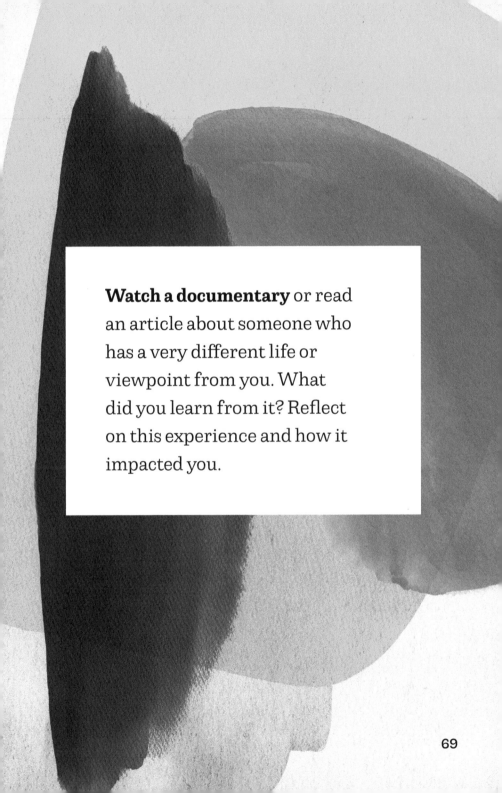

Watch a documentary or read an article about someone who has a very different life or viewpoint from you. What did you learn from it? Reflect on this experience and how it impacted you.

I am grateful for my happy memories because I get to relive the joy whenever I think about them.

One of my favorite memories is...

_____

_____

_____

_____

_____

_____

_____

_____

_____

_____

_____

_____

_____

_____

What is your fondest memory of an important person in your life?

_____

_____

_____

_____

_____

_____

_____

_____

Which of your senses evokes memories most strongly? Is it the smell of something? A song? A photo of a particular place? What feelings do they evoke and how can you tap into those emotions as part of your gratitude practice?

_____

_____

_____

_____

_____

_____

_____

_____

_____

On one day this week, choose a certain memory to honor or relive with someone you care about. Perhaps it's eating the same meal you had on your first date with your partner, or meeting up with your childhood best friend to do an activity you loved to do together as kids. Notice how you feel as you relive this memory and write about it in your journal.

You shouldn't rush…There are no taste buds in your stomach.

— ANTHONY MARRA

Describe your favorite meal and why you love it so much.

_____

_____

_____

_____

_____

_____

_____

_____

_____

_____

_____

_____

_____

_____

_____

_____

Do you prefer sweet, sour, or savory foods? Why?

_____

_____

_____

_____

_____

_____

_____

What was one of the most memorable meals you've had in your life? Describe all of the different flavors and textures and think about what made it so memorable. Where were you? Who were you with?

_____

_____

_____

_____

_____

_____

_____

_____

_____

Taste one new thing this week. Go to a new restaurant. Cook a new recipe. Buy something from the grocery store that you've never tasted before. Think about the excitement and anticipation of trying something new. Reflect on your experience in your journal.

I will take time each day
to smell the roses.

What is your favorite fragrance or smell and why?

_____

_____

_____

_____

_____

_____

_____

_____

_____

_____

_____

_____

_____

_____

_____

What is one scent that makes you nostalgic whenever you smell it and why?

_____

_____

_____

_____

_____

_____

_____

_____

Describe happiness as something you can smell. What does it smell like? Why does it remind you of happiness?

_____

_____

_____

_____

_____

_____

_____

_____

_____

Engage your sense of smell throughout the week. Light a scented candle, spray lavender on your pillow, use an essential oil diffuser, bake or cook something, smell flowers, or breathe in the fragrance of your morning coffee or tea. Think about how these scents make you feel.

Touch has a memory.

— JOHN KEATS

What is one thing that you can touch that always brings you comfort?

_____

_____

_____

_____

_____

_____

_____

_____

_____

_____

_____

_____

_____

_____

_____

_____

Name five objects or textures that you enjoy touching. What do you like about them? How do they make you feel?

_____

_____

_____

_____

_____

_____

Think about a time when a touch from someone was especially meaningful. What were the circumstances surrounding that touch? What did the touch convey to you?

_____

_____

_____

_____

_____

_____

_____

_____

_____

_____

This week, engage your sense of touch. Gather some things that have special meaning to you—maybe a shell you found on the beach or a hair ribbon from your childhood. Close your eyes and touch one of the items. As you hold the item, think about the memory associated with it and the feelings that come up. Do this with each of the items. Reflect on this experience.

You are never too old to set another goal or to dream a new dream.

— LES BROWN

What is a goal that you set for yourself that you were able to achieve, and what was it like to achieve it?

_____

_____

_____

_____

_____

_____

_____

_____

_____

_____

_____

_____

_____

_____

_____

Setting goals in my life helps me ...

_____

_____

_____

_____

_____

_____

What kind of goal-setter are you? Do you like to set small goals that you can achieve one after the other? Or do you prefer to set your sights on one big goal in the future? Do you like to share your goals with a trusted friend or keep them to yourself? How do you keep yourself accountable?

_____

_____

_____

_____

_____

_____

_____

_____

Think about a goal that you would like to achieve. Close your eyes and imagine yourself completing the necessary steps and accomplishing your goal. What is going on? Who is with you? How are you dressed? What do you see? What do you hear? What are you touching? What do you smell and taste? How does it feel? What did you enjoy most about this experience?

> My siblings are special to
> me, and I will always be
> there to support them.

I am grateful for my siblings, or someone who is like a sibling to me, because...

_____

_____

_____

_____

_____

_____

_____

_____

_____

_____

_____

_____

_____

_____

What is your favorite memory of your siblings, or someone who is like a sibling to you, and why?

_____

_____

_____

_____

_____

_____

_____

Describe the bond you have with your closest sibling, or someone who is like a sibling to you. Why is this relationship so meaningful to you, and why do you get along so well? What's something only they know about you?

_____

_____

_____

_____

_____

_____

_____

This week, find a way to show a sibling (or sibling figure) how much you appreciate your relationship. You could write them a letter or call them, cook them their favorite meal, or babysit their kids so that they can have some free time. If this isn't possible, share your appreciation with someone who knew your sibling figure and together, celebrate their memory. Reflect on this experience in your journal.

> I am a great communicator, and
> I use my voice to lift others up.

A time I spoke up for myself was when . . .

_____

_____

_____

_____

_____

_____

_____

_____

_____

_____

_____

_____

_____

_____

_____

_____

_____

A time I spoke up for someone else was when . . .

_____

_____

_____

_____

_____

_____

_____

_____

_____

Think about a time when you were able to soothe someone with your voice. How did you adjust your tone to make it comforting? What kinds of words did you use?

_____

_____

_____

_____

_____

_____

_____

_____

This week, use your voice. Talk to an old friend. Sing your favorite song. Express gratitude for others and think about the words you say and the emotions you feel. Notice how what you say affects others.

Life is a succession of lessons which must be lived to be understood.

— RALPH WALDO EMERSON

One of the most valuable lessons I ever learned was . . .

_____

_____

_____

_____

_____

_____

_____

_____

_____

_____

_____

_____

_____

_____

Name one person in your life who taught you many important lessons, and describe why you are so grateful to them.

_____

_____

_____

_____

_____

_____

_____

What is a lesson that you had to learn the hard way? What about this lesson was the most difficult? Why are you grateful for this lesson?

_____

_____

_____

_____

_____

_____

_____

_____

_____

This week, identify a young person in your life whom you think might benefit from some of your life lessons. Find a way to share those lessons by writing a letter or discussing them over a coffee or milkshake. Reflect on how it felt to pass on that wisdom.

My life is more satisfying when
I share my talents with others.

What is one talent that you admire and why?

_____

_____

_____

_____

_____

_____

_____

_____

_____

_____

_____

_____

_____

_____

What talent are you most proud of having and why?

_____

_____

_____

_____

_____

_____

_____

_____

What is a talent that you would like to develop? Why do you want
to cultivate that talent, and how would you go about it?

_____

_____

_____

_____

_____

_____

_____

_____

Choose one day this week when you put one of your talents to good use and share it with others. If you're a great baker, you could make cookies for your coworkers. If you have a green thumb, you could help your elderly neighbor with their garden. Focus on how it makes you feel to share your talent with others. Did you feel more connected to them?

We are what we repeatedly do. Excellence, then, is not an act, but a habit.

— ARISTOTLE

Describe your daily routine and what you like most about it.

_____

_____

_____

_____

_____

_____

_____

_____

_____

_____

_____

_____

_____

_____

_____

Having a routine helps me...

_____

_____

_____

_____

_____

_____

_____

_____

Think about your weekly routine and identify what is good about it and what needs improvement. What are three changes you can make to improve your routine?

_____

_____

_____

_____

_____

_____

_____

_____

Pick a day this week to practice mindfulness as you follow your routine. Notice what you are doing and what you are feeling while doing it. Engage all of your senses and ground yourself in the moment. When you notice yourself thinking about something else, direct your attention back to what you are doing. Reflect on this experience and how you felt afterward.

> I feel the warmth of the sunshine
> on my skin, and I am at peace.

How would you describe the way sunshine transforms an ordinary day?

_____

_____

_____

_____

_____

_____

_____

_____

_____

_____

_____

_____

_____

_____

On a sunny day, I like to . . .

_____

_____

_____

_____

_____

_____

_____

_____

_____

What are the top five reasons you are grateful for sunshine?

_____

_____

_____

_____

_____

_____

_____

_____

_____

_____

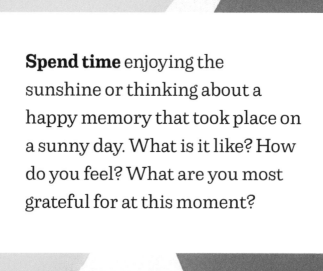

Spend time enjoying the sunshine or thinking about a happy memory that took place on a sunny day. What is it like? How do you feel? What are you most grateful for at this moment?

I am soothed by the rhythmic sound of the falling rain.

What is your favorite rainy-day memory?

_____

_____

_____

_____

_____

_____

_____

_____

_____

_____

_____

_____

_____

_____

Describe the kind of music you like to listen to on a rainy day and how it makes you feel.

_____

_____

_____

_____

_____

_____

_____

_____

Describe your ideal rainy day. Where are you? Whom are you with? What are you doing? What do you enjoy about it? How are you feeling?

_____

_____

_____

_____

_____

_____

_____

_____

_____

The next time it rains, embrace your inner child and play in it. Splash in the puddles and dance. Think about how it makes you feel and focus on the joyfulness of the moment.

> Reading helps me engage my
> imagination, expand my mind,
> and learn new things.

Describe your favorite childhood book and what you loved about it.

_____

_____

_____

_____

_____

_____

_____

_____

_____

_____

_____

_____

_____

_____

What is a book that you read recently that you are grateful for
and why?

_____

_____

_____

_____

_____

_____

_____

Think about something you read that changed the way you look at
the world. What did you learn? In what ways did it move you? Why
was it so meaningful?

_____

_____

_____

_____

_____

_____

_____

_____

_____

Pick one day this week and set aside an uninterrupted block of 30 minutes to read something that interests you. Think about what you are reading and what emotions come up. What does it feel like to schedule time and read something you enjoy? How could you make this a regular practice for yourself?

No borders, just horizons—only freedom.

— AMELIA EARHART

To me, freedom means...

_____

_____

_____

_____

_____

_____

_____

_____

_____

_____

_____

_____

_____

_____

_____

_____

What is a freedom or right that you are grateful for and why?

_____

_____

_____

_____

_____

_____

_____

_____

Describe five ways the concept of freedom has shaped your life.

_____

_____

_____

_____

_____

_____

_____

_____

_____

_____

As you go about your week, think
of all of the things you can do
because you are free. Consider
what aspects of your life would
be different without freedom.
Reflect on how this exercise
impacted you and how it makes
you view your life differently.

> I am grateful for travel and open to the new experiences that it brings.

What is one thing you like about travel and why?

_____

_____

_____

_____

_____

_____

_____

_____

_____

_____

_____

_____

_____

_____

_____

_____

Describe the most memorable trip you've taken and why it was so meaningful.

_____

_____

_____

_____

_____

_____

_____

_____

Think about a place you would like to travel to. Describe this place and what you would most like to do there.

_____

_____

_____

_____

_____

_____

_____

_____

_____

_____

Choose a day this week to take a trip to a nearby location that you have never been to before. It could be a different neighborhood or a nearby town. Research the area and decide what you want to do there. Consider whether it's a day trip or a weekend stay and when would be the best time to go. What will you take with you? Think about the anticipation and excitement that you feel as you plan your trip.

Life is so full of unpredictable beauty and strange surprises.

— MARK OLIVER EVERETT

Do you prefer giving or receiving surprises? Why?

_____

_____

_____

_____

_____

_____

_____

_____

_____

_____

_____

_____

_____

_____

What do you like most about surprising someone?

_____

_____

_____

_____

_____

_____

_____

Describe a favorite surprise you received. What did you like most about it? How do you feel when you think about it now?

_____

_____

_____

_____

_____

_____

_____

_____

_____

Plan a surprise for someone this week. You can write an anonymous note to tell someone how wonderful they are, surprise your family with a special dessert, or plan a fun day with someone special. Think about how you feel as you plan it—are you excited or nervous about how they will react? How did you feel afterward?

> I experience the world in a magical way when I view it through the eyes of a child.

What do you enjoy most about spending time with children?

_____

_____

_____

_____

_____

_____

_____

_____

_____

_____

_____

_____

_____

_____

In what ways do children view the world differently from adults, and how can you incorporate that perspective into your life?

_____

_____

_____

_____

_____

_____

_____

_____

Think about a meaningful experience you had with an important child in your life. Describe this experience and what it meant to you.

_____

_____

_____

_____

_____

_____

_____

_____

_____

Look at a photograph of yourself as a child. Think about what was going on and what you were feeling. What does this child need most? How can you comfort or encourage them? Pick one day this week to sit down and write them a letter to let them know how special, important, and loved they are.

The art of teaching is the art of assisting discovery.

— MARK VAN DOREN

Who was your favorite teacher and why?

_____

_____

_____

_____

_____

_____

_____

_____

_____

_____

_____

_____

_____

_____

Why are you grateful for teachers?

_____

_____

_____

_____

_____

_____

_____

How can you show appreciation for a teacher you know currently?
Perhaps it's a teacher of your child, niece, or nephew, or a friend
who is a teacher. Maybe it's your tennis coach or yoga instructor.
What do you think they would most like to hear?

_____

_____

_____

_____

_____

_____

_____

_____

_____

_____

_____

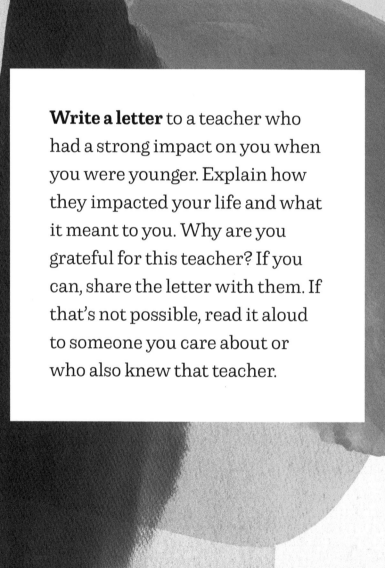

Write a letter to a teacher who had a strong impact on you when you were younger. Explain how they impacted your life and what it meant to you. Why are you grateful for this teacher? If you can, share the letter with them. If that's not possible, read it aloud to someone you care about or who also knew that teacher.

I enjoy watching a good movie that
inspires me and brings me joy.

What movie have you watched more than once and why?

_____

_____

_____

_____

_____

_____

_____

_____

_____

_____

_____

_____

_____

_____

_____

What movie reminds you of someone who is special to you
and why?

_____

_____

_____

_____

_____

_____

_____

_____

What is a movie that makes you feel strong emotions? What is it
about the plot or characters that touches you so much?

_____

_____

_____

_____

_____

_____

_____

_____

_____

Pick a night this week to watch a movie. You can rewatch one of your favorite movies or pick something new. Reflect on what you enjoyed about the movie and what you felt as you watched it. Did you laugh a lot? Were you inspired? Did it make you feel optimistic? Did you learn something new about the world?

Music can name the unnamable and communicate the unknowable.

— LEONARD BERNSTEIN

What is a song that always makes you feel good and why?

_____

_____

_____

_____

_____

_____

_____

_____

_____

_____

_____

_____

_____

_____

_____

What type of music do you like best, and what do you like about it?

_____

_____

_____

_____

_____

_____

_____

_____

Think about a song that brings up a strong memory. What is the song? Describe the memory. What feelings come up when you listen to this song?

_____

_____

_____

_____

_____

_____

_____

_____

This week, instead of listening to the music you usually listen to, ask a friend or loved one to recommend their favorite music. As you listen, notice how it makes you feel. What do you like about it? Does it evoke particular emotions? Does it make you want to dance? Is it relaxing or energetic? Why do you think that person likes this music so much?

I freely express my gratitude
and appreciation to myself
and everyone around me.

How do you know when someone appreciates you without them
telling you?

_____

_____

_____

_____

_____

_____

_____

_____

_____

_____

_____

_____

_____

_____

To show appreciation for someone else, I . . .

_____

_____

_____

_____

_____

_____

_____

_____

What do you appreciate most about yourself and why? What are
five ways you can show appreciation for yourself?

_____

_____

_____

_____

_____

_____

_____

_____

_____

_____

_____

Think about everyone and everything in your life that you appreciate. Consider why you appreciate them. Pick a day during the week to tell someone how much you appreciate them and why. Reflect on how it feels to focus on all of the good and share your appreciation.

'You changed' is a compliment.

— RACHEL HOLLIS

The most sincere compliment I've ever received was . . .

_____

_____

_____

_____

_____

_____

_____

_____

_____

_____

_____

_____

_____

_____

_____

_____

How do you feel when you give someone else a compliment, and why do you feel this way?

_____

_____

_____

_____

_____

_____

_____

Think about a compliment you received that was very meaningful to you. What was the compliment? Why was it so special to you?

_____

_____

_____

_____

_____

_____

_____

_____

_____

This week, think about the people you know—their good qualities and what you like about them. Pick a day to give someone in your life a sincere compliment. Give yourself a sincere compliment as well. Reflect on what doing this was like for you.

| Relaxing my body and mind is easy. |

To me, relaxation means...

_____

_____

_____

_____

_____

_____

_____

_____

_____

_____

_____

_____

_____

_____

_____

_____

Who makes you feel the most relaxed when you're with them and why?

_____

_____

_____

_____

_____

_____

_____

What are five things that help you relax, and why are they so relaxing?

_____

_____

_____

_____

_____

_____

_____

_____

_____

_____

Lie on your back in a comfortable position. Place one hand on your stomach and one hand on your chest. Slowly breathe in for a count of four, sending your breath down to your stomach so that it expands and your hand rises. Your chest should remain still. Tighten your abdominal muscles so your stomach contracts as you exhale for a count of seven. Do this for about five to ten minutes and reflect on how you feel after completing this exercise.

Daring to set boundaries is about having the courage to love ourselves, even when we risk disappointing others.

— BRENE BROWN

Boundaries are important because . . .

_____

_____

_____

_____

_____

_____

_____

_____

_____

_____

_____

_____

An experience in my life that taught me that I needed to set a
boundary was when...

_____

_____

_____

_____

_____

_____

_____

_____

Think about a boundary that is in place that you are very grateful
for. What is this boundary and why are you grateful for it?

_____

_____

_____

_____

_____

_____

_____

_____

_____

_____

Think about a boundary that you could establish to improve your well-being. Do you have trouble with your work-life balance? Do you always say yes, even when you want to say no? Do you feel as if someone is taking advantage of you? What is one small step you can take toward establishing a boundary? How will it be helpful? Once you've put it in place, reflect on how it feels to set a boundary for yourself.

I solve my problems easily when I follow my own advice.

The best advice I've ever received is...

_____

_____

_____

_____

_____

_____

_____

_____

_____

_____

_____

_____

_____

_____

_____

_____

Some helpful advice I have given someone is ...

_____

_____

_____

_____

_____

_____

_____

Think about a time when you faced a difficult situation and someone's advice helped you through it. What was the advice that you received? How did it help you?

_____

_____

_____

_____

_____

_____

_____

_____

_____

Consider a time that you were grateful for following your own advice instead of someone else's. Why are you grateful that you did this? How do you feel when you think about this?

There's nothing more intimate in life than simply being understood. And understanding someone else.

— BRAD MELTZER

A time I felt really understood was when...

_____

_____

_____

_____

_____

_____

_____

_____

_____

_____

_____

_____

_____

A time I really understood someone else was when . . .

_____

_____

_____

_____

_____

_____

_____

_____

Why is it important to be understood? How do you feel when someone really understands you? What does this level of understanding do for your relationship?

_____

_____

_____

_____

_____

_____

_____

_____

Gain a deeper understanding of yourself. Each night before bed this week, ask yourself a question that will help enhance your self-understanding and write your answers down. Questions could include:

- What qualities do you most admire in yourself?
- What are your biggest strengths?
- What are your dreams and goals? Why are they important to you?
- What are you most proud of?
- How would you describe yourself?
- When do you feel most at peace?

Reflect on your answers and how they enable you to gain a deeper understanding of yourself.

> When I look around me, I see
> inspiration everywhere.

I feel most inspired when ...

_____

_____

_____

_____

_____

_____

_____

_____

_____

_____

_____

_____

_____

_____

_____

What has been one of the greatest sources of inspiration in your life and why?

_____

_____

_____

_____

_____

_____

_____

_____

_____

Which five people inspire you most? How do they inspire you?

_____

_____

_____

_____

_____

_____

_____

_____

_____

One day this week, spend 15 minutes researching inspirational quotes on the internet. On a piece of paper or on your phone, write down the quotes that inspire you the most. Whenever you need a boost throughout the week, read one or two of the quotes. What do you think about when you read each quote? What does it mean to you? How does it inspire you?

Now and then it's good to pause in our pursuit of happiness and just be happy.

— GUILLAUME APOLLINAIRE

What are you thinking about in this very moment?

_____

_____

_____

_____

_____

_____

_____

_____

_____

_____

_____

_____

_____

_____

_____

How do you feel right now and why do you feel this way?

_____

_____

_____

_____

_____

_____

_____

_____

_____

Look around you and list 10 things that you are grateful for in this moment. Explain why you are grateful for these things.

_____

_____

_____

_____

_____

_____

_____

_____

_____

Pick a morning this week to meditate for one minute and focus on that moment. Sit in a comfortable position, set a timer, and focus on breathing in through your nose and out through your mouth. When your mind wanders, simply notice your thoughts without judgment. Bring your attention back to your breath and the sensation of inhaling and exhaling. Reflect on your experience.

I am grateful for myself.

What do you like most about yourself?

_____

_____

_____

_____

_____

_____

_____

_____

_____

_____

_____

_____

_____

_____

_____

_____

_____

What is your proudest accomplishment?

_____

_____

_____

_____

_____

_____

_____

_____

Write a love letter to yourself. Describe all the reasons that you are grateful for being you and what makes you special.

_____

_____

_____

_____

_____

_____

_____

_____

_____

_____

Each night this week, think of one thing that you did well that day or were happy about. Reflect on what happened and what you appreciate about it.

Resources

BOOKS

The Psychology of Gratitude by Robert E. Emmons and Michael McCullough

A Simple Act of Gratitude by John Kralik

MOBILE APPS

Gratitude for iOS and Android

365 Gratitude for iOS and Android

PODCASTS

The Gratitude Podcast by Georgian Benta, GeorgianBenta.com

The Positive Psychology Podcast by Kristen Truempy

WEBSITES

A Network for Grateful Living, Gratefulness.org

Positive Psychology, PositivePsychology.com

References

Angelou, Maya. *All God's Children Need Traveling Shoes*. New York: Random House, 1986.

Apollinaire, Guillaume. "Guillaume Apollinaire Quotes." Goodreads. Goodreads.com/quotes/24892-now-and-then-it-s-good-to-pause-in-our-pursuit.

Aquinas, Thomas. "Thomas Aquinas." *Wikiquote*. Accessed February 16, 2021. En.wikiquote.org/wiki/Thomas_Aquinas.

Aristotle. "Aristotle." *Wikiquote*. Accessed February 18, 2021. En.wikiquote.org/wiki/Aristotle.

Bernstein, Leonard. *The Unanswered Question: Six Talks at Harvard*. Cambridge: Harvard University Press, 1981.

Brown, Brene. Brene Brown: 3 Ways to Set Boundaries. Oprah.com. Accessed May 10, 2021. https://www.oprah.com/spirit/how-to-set-boundaries-brene-browns-advice#.

Brown, Les. *Live Your Dreams*. New York: William Morrow, 1992.

Byron, Lord. "Lord Byron." *Wikiquote*. Accessed February 18, 2021. En.wikiquote.org/wiki/Lord_Byron.

Earheart, Amelia. Quotetab. Accessed May 10, 202. https://www.quotetab.com/quotes/by-amelia-earhart.

Eliot, George. *Mr. Gilfil's Love Story*. London: Hesperus Press, 1857.

Emmons, Robert A., and Michael E. McCullough. "Counting Blessings Versus Burdens: An Experimental Investigation of Gratitude and Subjective Well-Being in Daily Life." *Journal of Personality and Social Psychology* 84, no. 2 (February 2003): 377–389, https://doi.org/10.1037//0022-3514.84.2.377.

Everett, Mark Oliver. *Things the Grandchildren Should Know*. New York: Little, Brown, 2007.

Grant, Adam M., and Francesca Gino. "A Little Thanks Goes A Long Way: Explaining Why Gratitude Expressions Motivate Prosocial Behavior." *Journal of Personality and Social Psychology* 98, no. 6 (2010): 946–955, https://doi.org/10.1037/a0017935.

Hobb, Robin. *Fool's Fate*. New York: Bantam Spectra, 2004.

Hollis, Rachel. "OF course you changed!" Facebook, September 5, 2019. Facebook.com/TheChicSite/photos/a.199476321258/10157285793646259/?-type=3&theater.

Hughes, Langston. *The Dream Keeper and Other Poems*. New York: Alfred A. Knopf, 1932.

CONTINUED »

References CONTINUED

Keats, John. *The Poetical Works of John Keats*. London: Taylor and Walton, 1871.

Lorde, Audre. *Sister Outsider: Essays and Speeches*. Berkeley, CA: Ten Speed Press, 1984.

Marra, Anthony. *A Constellation of Vital Phenomena*. New York, NY: Random House Publishing Group, 2014.

McLaren, Karla. *The Language of Emotions: What Your Feelings are Trying to Tell You*. Louisville, CO: Sounds True, Inc., 2010.

McMahon, Daniel. *The Little Book of Medical Quotes: Inspiring Thoughts in Medicine*. Shropshire, UK: TFM Publishing Limited, 2020.

Meltzer, Brad. *The Inner Circle*. New York, NY: Grand Central Publishing, 2011.

Tolstoy, Leo. *Pamphlets*. Translated from the Russian. Christchurch, Hants: Free Age Press, 1900.

University of California, Berkeley, Greater Good Science Center. *Thnx4*. Accessed February 15, 2021. Thnx4.org.

Van Doren, Mark. Goodreads. Accessed May 10, 2021. https://www.goodreads.com/author/quotes/187663.Mark_Van_Doren.

Walls, Laura Dassow. *Henry David Thoreau: A Life*. Chicago: University of Chicago Press, 2017.

About the Author

Keir Brady, MS, LMFT, is a marriage and family therapist in private practice. She works with couples and individuals to help them turn their relationship and personal struggles into life-enhancing opportunities for growth. Through practicing gratitude and focusing on the positive,, Keir helps couples improve their connection, and individuals enhance their emotional well-being. She is a featured expert in the documentary film *Lessons in Forgiveness*. Keir lives in the Atlanta area with her family, including two dogs, Hansen and Rocco, and tortoise, Fred. To learn more about Keir, visit KeirBradyCounseling.com.

CPSIA information can be obtained
at www.ICGtesting.com
Printed in the USA
BVHW050732140921
616219BV00005BA/2

9 781648 767296